OBSERVATORY

ALISON J SCHULTZ

authorHOUSE®

AuthorHouse™ UK
1663 Liberty Drive
Bloomington, IN 47403 USA
www.authorhouse.co.uk
Phone: UK TFN: 0800 0148641 (Toll Free inside the UK)
    UK Local: 02036 956322 (+44 20 3695 6322 from outside the UK)

Published by AuthorHouse 12/18/2020

ISBN: 978-1-6655-8362-6 (sc)
ISBN: 978-1-6655-8361-9 (e)

PREFACE

This is my second volume of poetry, and I set myself the challenge of looking for a different source of inspiration; to actively seek out stories, images and experiences to write about, rather than waiting for the poems to come on their own. This search took various forms.

One was to ask people I encountered for moments, and this brought some real gems. Another was to sit and watch people pass, a situation for which I am particularly suited because I have MS and use a mobility scooter. In addition, my husband and I are musicians, and some lovely moments came from festivals, street corners and chats.

The truth is that daily life is a richly abundant source of stories and inspiration, and I did not have to look very hard. I hope you enjoy the outcome and I would very much welcome feedback at <u>www.facebook.com/alisonjschultzpoetry</u>

A good friend, who is an engineer, said that to simply read the poems for himself was like giving him sheet music and expecting it to come to life: he only really "got it" when he heard me reading. To hear me reading the poems for you please follow the link.

Paper Souls

The gold edged leaves of books
Are the rustling souls of trees;
Their voice speaks at a page turn;
Each word is wind-whispered
And to place them on shelves
Is to send them home to the wood.
Yet in the hands of a child or lover
Of other lives, the turning pages
Unfurl their magic, and even at night
In the unlit libraries or under bed covers
Their myriad voices swirl in murmurations.

Viral

Out in the dusky garden, among the flowers
And the fairy lights, the gentle fountain-trickle,
The air is startlingly quiet, free of air traffic,
Rippled only by an occasional car on empty roads.
Each liquid cascade of notes from the throats of birds
Is, at last, given its due gravitas...echoing, hanging
In the moment. This newly quiet air of our busy silly world
Is a beautiful gift and a clarion call to re-assess our excess;
We would not stop, rushing headlong toward disaster.
Disaster came, and now we must. We are constrained
By the Law, to read, to connect, to sit in our gardens at dusk
And truly hear the loveliness of the world with which we gambled.

The Sounds of our Land

Bring back to me the wild whisper of the waves;
The slurp and rattle of a pebbly shore pulled
Back and forth, into ridge and slope and cave.
Bring back to me the last blackbird before sundown
Pouring shimmering notes through the darkening air
Into the cathedral echo of the velvet gloaming.
Bring to me the tractor-sound, labouring over rise
And furrow of rich soil, and the rustle of wet wellies
And dog paws through lush long grasses and mud,
Or the first cuckoo calling out across the meadows
As Spring scatters dainty flutters of wildflowers.

How to sift my ears through all the precious sounds
Of my dear river-compassed lovely piece of land?
The wind in my ear is the voice of my beloved;
The seal-songs, the lonely curlews on the marsh,
Train-echoes across the wide estuary from Wales,
As utterly familiar to me as the beating of my heart.

Shackleton's List

Snowed under with letters from aspirational adventurers
In ill-disciplined drifts on table, desk, bureau and carpet,
With a schedule threatened by competition and by war,
And funding impossible, he fixed his weather-squint eyes
On climbing a glacier of preparation. First, choose a team.
Men first, before ship, rations, sled dogs, tents and equipment.

His carefully-worded advert had striven for discouraging realism;
Yet the responders varied wildly, and must be combined well, or die.
He read them, then read again. After a week, three piles emerged;
Those who would be reckless glory-seekers, risking the team;
Those who had proved themselves utterly ignorant of the challenge;
And, at last, the Alpinists, experienced with endurance and danger.
Three piles for an expedition to make history.
Mad, hopeless, and possible.

Harvest

Her Mother always said that Autumn made her sad
As the sun set sooner, and the fields turned to bronze.
Her younger self had gloried in the blaze of crimson,
Russet, amber, as the leaves flushed and fluttered,
Fruit hung heavy, and the scent of the soil like cocoa;
The whole point of seed, and growth, and planting.

But as she herself tipped past full bloom, sensing
At last the breath of longer nights and shorter days,
And seeing her neck and the fine backs of her hands
Start to wrinkle and dry, like apples stored on shelves,
She understood her Mother's preference for summer,
Where faces are like flowers turned to the warm sun,
And many long days are on offer before the Dark comes.

Harvest Moon

There is the power of the Old Ways tonight
In the clarity of the sky over threshed fields
Where silvered light pours down on stack
And on stubble; where owl and fox stalk
And flit from shadow to shadow, and mice hide.
The year has safely blossomed, grown, fruited.
Bramble and fat rose-hips, Rowan, heavy apples
Have had their moments. Striped spiders
Spin webs across every corner with their silk.
Above it all; the Moon. Haloed, gracious, complete.

Chet Baker at first light

3am on a summer night, where the fingertips of Dawn
Touch the flickering eyelids of those who sleep too lightly
Or those who wake, and then are circled by vulture thoughts
And look out into quiet gardens for soft elusive solace.
Sent by a friend, then, a perfect shared soundtrack for all
Who sit in their beds reluctantly woken; Leaving, with Chet
Pouring delicate regretful trumpet against Bass elegance.
The web of the tune casts its silver threads into the night;
Connects sender, audience, players, in times of disconnection,
Making us all less lonely in our isolated Dawn wakefulness.

The Sunflowers of Passignano

When the sun has risen and set a thousand times
Across the faces of generations of Italian sunflowers,
And you have delightedly explored the further reaches
Of each other and this lovely earth; taking a chance,
Or soup on car windscreens, or the hurt and healing
Of your hearts and your patients' ills, or drowsy mornings
Dreaming of ripening vines and children calling in play;
All of this perfection of shared history and heartfelt hoping
Will be placed on a wide table shaded from the heat of the sun,
Where beloved faces will smile. And the beautiful question
Asked on a white beach where turtles swam in the waves
Will be answered. When is Love not a step into the uncharted?
It is braver than crossing the world, or healing the sick,
Or planting a thousand sunflowers and waiting for gold

For Vicki and Eduardo di Cuffa 30/05/2019

Freefall

This is what it feels like; only the fierce air
Rushing past out-stretched gloved fingers
Tugging insistently at starfished legs and feet
Invisibly pouring past goggles and helmet.
The silence is total save what sounds like Niagara.
Shreds of cloud veil the ground. The fields are green.
Only the grab and tug of my own hand can change
The outcome here; smash and tumble into fragments.
Or pull, and feel the savage uplift of the harness;
Glide down as hoped – or be obliterated in a second.
My choice. Find the energy to pull. Or wait too long.

Turn your face away

How could that work on the sardine-can tube trains
Where the workers are suddenly required to risk lives?
Or in a half-filled brightly painted classroom of tiny tots
Who will have to be re-programmed not to share or care,
Or risk carting home the Plague to hitherto safe homes?
What of their teachers and carers...of their families too?
Westminster is turning its bloated and privileged face
Away from them all, and about to ask the true heroes
To take a pay cut to foot the bill, as well as risk their lives,
Rather than retrieving uncollected taxes from billionaires
Hiding out of reach on their islands, while their country
Coughs and shrivels, and their leaders flounder on.

Mags

The light lay like pink pearls across the Mersey
Seen down a steep green slope made by a bomb
Seventy years ago, but yesterday to the pub that saw it.
Built to last 2 centuries ago and still serving,
A series of cosy parlours with firm benches,
Low ceilings where the layers of paint still clearly show
The wide oak boards of the floor above. Settled.

The building faces a river which once thronged with ships
And the broad bay windows have seen it all come
And go. Years ago, we played for a fancy dress party here
To celebrate 2 centuries; we came round the corner
To see Admirals and their Ladies, wigged and uniformed
Gathered outside. It was like a time slip; I loved it.

The huge stone door step dips from Time's footfall
And inside every room is packed with like-minded people.
We spend an evening turning fast tunes and slow songs
And bantering, laughing, tossing ideas back and forth.
It is like an old friend, this pub, to a great many people;
And it ain't done yet.

Weaver of spells

Fragile heart and fragile frame
But the mind of a magician, spinning
Silken strings of wisdom-pearls
In perfect patterns, like cobwebs
Dew-decked with the Autumn mist.
The shapes and patterns are there
For all, and yet pour from her soul
To catch us spellbound with her words.

For Colleen

Conversation in the woods

Under the ground the trees are talking,
Humming unseen through the woodland.
Little saplings get their share whooshed in
From towering parent high in the canopy,
And scientists have identified Mother trees
Who nourish their communities. Oh yes, they talk.

Fifty years ago, the native population of Australia
Were counted as Flora and Fauna; only arrogance
Prevents us hearing other, more subtle conversations
Among the beautiful and wise with whom we share;
Tread gently along the hollow forest floor; let your ears
And your heart listen, for all that it does not yet know.

Definition of communication; the imparting or sharing of
information.

Faded

Nothing makes you tired like lack of joy
Where sleep's a kind escape, and all that's sweet of life
Is on high shelves, without a ladder near.
Even human touch, or music-swell, or lovely waves
Smoothing down rough pebbles on the shore
Cannot smooth down the cares which so like boulders seem
To my sad heart. The days are over-long
Though light is short. Food tastes like dust or ash
And geese honk through the sky, turning their arrow heads
To warmer climes. Everything smells of loss;
Of age, not patina, where all the colour fades
On leaf and cheek and in bright eyes. The air feels thick
To my tired legs, where they push along as if through mud;
My mission, lost. I stumble on. I stumble on.

Sextant

Murmur of deepest ocean under my feet
Deeper than any man can dive down
Fathom below fathom, blue into black,
Where whole species of strange creatures
Live beyond the limits of our feeble knowing.
I feel your sway through my bones, and walk it
Even when I am an out-of-water fish on dry land.

We have circled the Globe, in uncharted waters,
We men from an Island nation of salty seafarers;
The craftsmen who shaped our ship with their hearts
Sent us out to trade, explore, discover, destroy.
Under us, the wild sea moves. Her storms pound,
The castles of the waves fierce and destructive.
Yet without the commands of the Silver Lady,
The sea would not move. It would be blown
But not drive, not direct. The stars are so distant
They may have been dead for millennia upon millennia
Before we even see them. And yet, with this Sextant
Made of wood and lens and ivory, I can use them.
With my Mistress the Ocean and the miraculous stars,
I can find my way home; until the tide pulls me back.

Padlocks and chains

All along the edge of the enormous Dock Wall
Where muscular Mersey waters shoulder up,
Bollards of forged iron and granite, weighty,
Joined three rows high by chunky Marine chain.
On almost every link, padlocks of every size;
Names, dates, messages, promises of love.
These are the records of wedding vows, or memories,
Locked into the chains on the docks of a port
Built by the Slave Trade. This is a different thing;
Enslavement to fidelity, to a beautiful idea
Of lasting love, with the hasp snapped shut
For ever, and the keys tossed into the river
To sink into the silt. What will they make of this,
The archaeologists of the future, all these keys?
Tens of thousands of locked-on promises of love
Preserved long after those who made them are gone.

Permanent

He opened his eyes drunk with joy and dawn light
And the dream was real. Honour had made no difference
At the last, and it was clear there was no going back.
Her smile bloomed in her eyes and clothed her all day
As they pottered about as if with vertigo; dizzy, dazed.
He told her he loved her more than Life, though later
She knew fear as she realised both halves of his words.
And later still, he wrote her answer in curly script above
their bed;
"I love you beyond reason or hope of redemption."

Washing Line

Helping out her daughter her washing line is full;
Remarkable in these days of hasty hot driers
Where the laundry smells cooked instead of fresh
And goes straight back in the drawers.
This line has fifty dazzling white tiny baby items
Snapping creases out (and sunshine in) in the breeze.

How can a baby make so much washing?
Smallest person in the family needing the most
As they always have. But just one generation ago
Before marvellous household machines arrived
And made it easy, laundry took most of the week
To soak, scrub, dry and iron. If it was raining, worse still;
Hanging on the airer round the coal fire, taking all the heat,
Steaming condensation onto the single-glazed panes.
Windy days were best, up and out, basket on her hip,
Peg between her teeth. All that sweet stretchy easy-care stuff
Now that it takes so little time, and so little time
Goes to the tiny ones while both parents go out to work.

Vaporised

The fly boys and girls are all grounded
Tin-can preposterous toys parked in rows
On silent tarmac. The shuttered perfumeries
And wine merchants line the marble halls,
Abandoned temples to disposable income
Or to International workplaces. Next to one such,
The ancient beams of a 500 year old manor
Relax smugly into the silence, and are peopled again
By those wearing velvet doublets and paniered gowns
While no-one is looking. Foxes play on the runways
And the air smells of Spring rather than jet fuel.

Up above, the skies are crossed only by flocks of birds
Above whom, the uninterrupted altitude of perfect azure
Stretches infinitely, free of vapour trail ribbons crossing
In distant embroideries which spell pollution and greed.

Arena

Leaving late from a large gig in a warm limo
He saw two middle-aged women racing full pelt
On mobility scooters, opposite ways to each other
Round a small roundabout, in the floodlit dark.
They were howling with laughter and waving;
It was a glimpse of unbridled joy, and proof
That joy can be entirely unrelated to good health
Or to youth, or kind circumstances.
It never left him.

Darien Chest

Before Banks or Safes there were chests.
Solid iron, and girded in further iron, weighty
With fortune as well as gold coin or jewels,
Too heavy for half a dozen strong men to heft,
Ferociously guarded under heavy lock and key.
Thieves of resource were countered by locksmiths
Who could devise, with what must have been joy,
Locks of devilish cunning, of perfect puzzledom;
Levers and cogs and teeth to bite burglarious men;
Locks which filled the entire underside of the lid.

One such marvel was lugged across the wide world
To create the bank of a Colony doomed to failure
And return home secure but empty of any gold
Ransacked by fate in spite of the best of endeavors...
Like the guarded treasure of many a lost heart.

The Darien Chest can be seen in the National Museum of Scotland
in Edinburgh

Pearl

For three shifts of midwives, she twisted and toiled,
Their faces passing her in a blur of sweat and fear.
Most of all she hated the relentlessness of the waves
Squeezing her with the grip of a giant or vengeful god.
Time lost all meaning but for the lungfuls of air in gaps,
Gasped into her burning chest before the next squeeze.
Shreds of her carefully chosen music reached her ears
And the life-line of hands that held hers through the pain.

At last she started to drift in between, numbed by effort
To the point where she would have been lost a century before.
There were ominous scurryings in the room, more staff,
The ring of authority in a new voice. Still, the storm came.
Brisk instructions, finally, gave her new will to engage;
There was a release, more effort, then a sudden wrench;
Then someone's kind voice said, "Her skin is like a pearl!"
And a part-wrapped bundle with huge eyes was placed
On her creaking gasping chest. And her heart was utterly lost.

Aber Soch

Out of the window the horizon is wide.
Trees stand with lacy arms upstretched,
And under the hedge, bulbs lift sleepy heads.
The clouds shift subtly, shimmering grey and pearl
With little scattered hints of blue and sunshine.
Through the open window, air is clean and cool.
Under it all, there is the quiet breathing of the sea.

The sea, the sky, the glimpse of Spring in the neat garden;
The gulls that swoop and call in their lofty playground;
The dark line where the feathers of the clouds cease,
And the moving pewter of the Irish Sea's smooth swell starts;
Healing, immense, swaying her crinoline waves with her dance;
Air currents that sound like the stately flaps of huge wings;
Under it all, there is the quiet breathing of the sea.

Teabags in the toaster

Our neighbour's mind is beginning to unravel.
She has been lively and independent until now,
Walking briskly every day in the fresh air
Chatty but not invasive, able to look after herself.
But now, quite suddenly, she is tipping; and she knows it.
Each day, small things seem to go wrong in the house;
The key won't go in the door, the TV is not responding,
And yesterday, a small fire after teabags in the toaster.
Hard to tell for how long it has been sliding away
But she is afraid now. She is onto the change in herself.
What could be worse? There can be no happy end
To this game, no easy solution to the melting of the mind.
Words are vanishing, lines of thought fracturing and lost;
The stories loop and repeat within minutes.

She sat drinking tea and her eyes showed flickers
Of panic, darting from side to side, no longer safe.
Someone, or something, is standing on the porch
Of her mind, waiting silently outside her door.
She does not want to look into its face. Who would?

Not just yet

Such a strong true heart, this silky little one,
Staying as close as ever with a ball in her chops
As her breath fails, tail still faintly waving
Resting her tired head, bony now, on my foot.

You have walked steadily beside me, dear friend,
Through a Tsunami of change and challenge.
You brought nothing with you but joy and faith.
Will you not cease the fight soon, let the tide flow?
Though I want to be parted from you
As little as you seem to want to go.

Pulling down statues

Toppling the leviathan statues
Of previous Dictators cannot undo
The wreckage of an economy, or find
The lost, or the incarcerated, or mend hearts
Shredded by cruelties. History cannot be erased;
It will still record their deeds, and our votes;
And we are as ants under the boots of Power.

Highwaymen

Where is the perceived glamour in thievery?
Stand and Deliver or the Pirates' fluid Code
With tricorns and braided Frock Coats and pistols
Swinging aboard or gallantly handing the lady out
Onto the deserted moonlit road, or Sherwood Forest
Where savage taxation gets confiscated and salvaged...

Wake up, you fools! Now, they read your opened mail,
Set quizzes online that feed them all your particulars,
Make plausible phone calls and keep you talking
While they hack your Banking App. Exactly now,
They are doing this to people living in fear of the Virus,
To those without work or food, who ricochet from loan
To Card, and back. But they are doing it to the busy ones,
The canny ones, the web-wise; those people too. Maybe you.

Dunstanburgh

Coarse grass combed by the fingers of the wind
Crunched under their feet. The brisk air and waves
Busied themselves among black rocks and seals,
And the dog's ears flowed back as he trotted ahead.
The ruins stood on a rise, the shape of the keep still
And the towers with their arrow slits and arches.
Inside, the sky and the sound of the sea were more
Than the perseverance of the walls. And the echoes;
Clear resonances of the breath of History; of cooks,
Of servants and their Lords, of the braw fighting men
Who watched the sea for the Norsemen in their boats;
Not haunted, no, but not done with the voices and lives
Of those whose minds remain in the fabric of the walls
And whose story curls in the wind through what still stands.

Who was John Bush?

Ancestry rummaging is a battered trunk
Inside which lie verified anecdotes and dust.
Dig down through one side and find 250 acres
Near Stirling, and deeper down warrior Dukes
Beyond the Norman Conquest. A castle, now ruined,
And a freedom-fighter ArchBishop of Scotland,
Kilted in tartan of their Clan, scattered to Ayrshire.
Even a less safe time in The Gorbals of Glasgow,
And three generations of passionate engineers.

But buried in the other corner lie the surprises;
Harder to trace further back without education.
Blacksmiths from County Kildare with big families,
Over to England in 1851 after the Great Famine,
To work in the shipyards, striking iron and steel.
Then in 1901, the lodger John Bush appears.
Research suggests he became known by their name
For "decency's sake" as no recorded marriage exists
Though the name change pops up in the Census.
Once, a letter came for John Bush, and was whisked
Out of the baffled hand of his re-named son's daughter.
Where is the first wife of John Bush? Left behind?
They used to call it the "Glad Eye", that saucy twinkle,
Passed down but later lost with his sight and sense of joy,
Leaving him huddled in a chair by the kitchen hearth
To be superceded by his handsome son in the charm stakes.

Until we meet again

His wife sat three days by their marital bed
Holding his hand, as she had every day for years.
The hands of the clock ticked in the quiet room
Like the last grains of sand sifting through the gap.
His familiar face was mostly without expression
Yet once in a while, would flicker with emotion
As a baby's does, when they are too small to know.
Mostly it felt as if he were sleeping, or perhaps absent.

Quite suddenly, as the afternoon sun lay on the floor,
His dear eyes opened; his dear face woke up, lit up.
His gaze was fixed on the other side of the room
Where she could see only a bland blank wall,
Though the joy in him made her strain to share it.
"The most beautiful thing I ever saw." he said,
And in the next breath, was gone from her.
But her loving heart felt warmed and calmed
That he felt thus about his next destination
And glad of the thought of, one day, meeting again.

Words of Fire

In my dream my arms are seared like steak
With words of fire; anger and betrayal and regret,
Blurred along the margins of the letters by melted skin.
Waking, flailing, trying to read the fury of the nightmare
Before it fades, as even the worst of them do, in daylight.
Are these my truth, burrowed, buried in my polite kindness?
Have I lived nearly six decades with a warrior dragon woman
Chained in the caves of my heart, subdued by my choosing
To forgive? As dawn breathes dew on the quiet grass blades,
And small creatures tuck away, my arms are once more whole,
Miraculously smoothed by my determined gaze. I know the beast.
I hear her roar, feel her lust for vengeance and destruction burn;
The cave is deep. I will never let her out. But I know she is there.

Dreams of White Horses

He enjoyed outfacing fear and spent much time
Being patched up repeatedly through childhood.
But when he was about twelve he found himself
Lying face down, unable to move and vomiting,
Half way over an unsteady suspension bridge
Across to a lighthouse. His instincts beat him
Because there is a difference between the drop
From a tree, and that from a cliff or from the sky.

So he discovered flying, and climbing mountains,
And when his back stopped co-operating for while
He learned to paint and showed an exhibit Entitled Vertigo.
He was not without fear; but it lost.

Years later he was clinging with curled chalky fingers
To an overhang on a craggy route poetically named
Dreams of White Horses by the climber who led it;
Hundreds of feet through empty air below his feet
The spray hurled itself at the rocks. And he recalled
With crystalline clarity that point of adolescent terror
Which was just around the headland, but a lifetime ago.

Ice cream Queens

Remember that gorgeous 50s pic of two girls,
Perched with ice creams on a beach railing,
With their full circle skirts doing a modest Marilyn?
Their coiffures? The laughing red-lippy mouths?
The simple Summer joy of jolly donkey days...
Today I sat and watched two feisty old biddies
Re-enacting the same story on their Zimmers
Best floral shirtwaists and a glimpse of knee- highs,
Ankles flopping over their Velcro shoes; but the same
General merriment caused by sea air and Mr Whippy
Complete with a nice flake and raspberry sauce.
And the same lovely sense of innocent naughtiness
That made me grin to myself as they trundled away

The Late Shift

Once in a while, there can be a moment
With the opening bars, where the room pauses.
The escalating convivial words and looks
Flutter like glitter or dust in the spotlight
Caught as in a shaken snow-globe. Time halts.
The start; a slinky vibration of bass, athletic guitar,
A vocal like warm honey or butter. Masters all.
And even if it is only an instant, stretched out
Like a cat on a wide windowsill, each one there
Will keep that spotlit snapshot in there for always.

The Ghost Light

The caretaker does his last round locking doors
After all the gaudy glamour and illusion are done;
Down the dark and dusty corridor with its echoes
Jostling past each other, to and from the stage,
With its lingering stink of sweat and greasepaint,
Grubby vinyl tiles scarred by the wheels of rails
Where the costumes had hung for quick changes.

He locks doors, flicks off light switches as he goes.
Last of all, the old ritual among the superstitious players;
Out through the wings onto the darkened deserted stage,
Faced by row upon row of empty seats and gilded boxes,
Hearing in his head the roar of applause and cheering.
He pushes the button to sweep across the heavy curtains,
And switches on the single naked bulb above the stage.
The Ghost Light will stay lit while the theatre is closed,
This time for months upon months while the virus rages,
And the ghosts of the famous strut and proclaim in peace.

The great Divide

Wirral is a scenic and lovely place, sharply demarcated.
To the West, facing the hills of Snowdonia across the Dee,
The salt marsh is gradually claiming the wide estuary
And flocks of birds swoop and chatter and winter over.
Here the pretty little towns are quaint and prosperous,
Fields are green and trimmed by ancient hedges and woods.
The main road runs like a curved ribbon each to each,
And the air is quiet and scented with faint salt and wind.

Over on the other side of this contained peninsular
There is the muscular and majestic river Mersey.
From Seacomb Ferry, each side of this great waterway
Is bordered by grotty Industry and manufacturing.
Then, from the Victorian elegance of Egremont Parade,
There are those breathtaking views across to the city.
There are pockets of great poverty and abandonment
Like sad social fungus, where the people struggle on
Helpless against joblessness and overwhelmed by torpor
When less than five miles away there is great wealth.
Both have their stories, like the Country in miniature,
With breathtaking perfections and blasts of grimness.

Burning

The recycle bin is overflowing
Still heading for landfill without us knowing
Tetra packs, glossy mags, cartons and bags
Chewing gum, PVC, filters from fags,
Our greedy short-sightedness comes at a cost;
And now the Amazon is burning.

Factories roar toxins with dragon fury
Nuclear waste buried; another story
Whole species deleted, forests depleted
For poisonous Palm-oil, the story's repeated.
Our greedy short-sightedness is melting the ice;
And now the Amazon is burning.

This beautiful world has a generous supply
Of all that we need, and plenty put by;
Enough for us all if only shared round
The trade made of goods, instead of the Pound.
Our greedy short-sightedness has gone on too long.
And now the Amazon is burning.

Lost in his own museum

Each day he drags up his aging creaking bones
Quietly goes by the wide window in the wing chair
And, as the afternoon sun warms his paper skin,
He leans back his head, shuts his eyes, dreams.
Inside his mind, the archive of his precious life
Is laid out like treasures, to be revisited and loved.
He opens the shuttered windows to summer birdsong,
Leans down, limber in this gentler place, lifts memory
After memory out. Sunny river picnics from childhood;
Lying tipsy on love and ale in a meadow, head in her lap;
Turning to look at her through his own tears – his bride.
The miraculous blood and agony of birth, and its result,
And the accelerated magic lantern of the growth of each
Of their precious perfect children; years flying past years.
Each afternoon he naps, lost in the beautiful museum
Of his own life, where his past is more real than his chair.

Valeria

The day she went
We looked at the sea
The sky was inappropriately wide and bright;
Dazzling clusters of gossiping gulls
Sat about on the sand.
Up in the blue, streamers of chiffon cloud
Wafted about, as from a dancer's arm.
I loved her. My choices severed us
From one another;
I felt, and feel, the pain of that
Like a missing limb.
Years and years of laughter and shared time
There still in pictures of the heart.

Straw and Velvet

The narrow streets were still jostling into the evening;
A thousand feet over the slippery ancient cobblestones.
Small carts with wooden wheels rumbled under arches
And oil lamps glowed in the deep set window holes.
Hours passed, folk got settled. Heavy doors grated shut.
The small, over-stuffed town hunkered down for the night.
Some had come far, and needed many stops. Her bump
Had ached and necessitated breaks. They were late.
No matter; after many knocks a kind soul made space.
The animals warmed the night air and the straw was fresh.
Her quiet struggle through the pain was filled with dignity
That created peace from dirt, and he did his best to help.
Afterwards, he made her a nest close to the feed box
And she lay back and gazed on the beauty of the child
Who gazed back with wise old eyes. Through tatty thatch
The starlight glowed, as strange visitors came and went.
Observing her from a dim corner, she met each with grace,
Whether filthy sheep herders or brocaded foreigners.
Somehow the borrowed smelly space was a court
And she the lovely queen of it with her weary eyes.
At last it was quiet, and the velvet dark settled over them,
He with his arms round her, and hers round the sleepy child.

Punishment

We can take a fair bit, we can.
But...lying flat on your back
With the paving slabs stacked
On your chest, ribs cracking
Organs compressing, crushed.
One slab is heavy, two is worse.
Then another, another, more.
Stone and stone and stone, on me.

Blacksmith

Unchanging soundtrack of hoof on cobbles,
Of hammer blow against unflinching anvil;
And spark-smell, bellows-belch, steam-hiss;
Iron, the stuff of legends, commanded and shaped
By men of muscle and skill, makers of tools
When the hammer was all things to all men;
Both tool and weapon. The forge still stands,
Dressed in oaken beams, at the fork of the road,
Where church and village hall form a triangle.
Between wide doors a man of iron works on,
Smiting glowing metal; twist, and smite again,
Each mighty blow reverberating through history;
Through Ley Lines, and Standing Stones and family trees.

The First to Hear the News

Seb's great-great-grandfather was from Liverpool.
He got a fine moment in history, as fine as it gets;
His were the first ears to hear (in Morse Code)
The first eyes to read, fingers to trace That Message.
The year is 1918. He is the first to know in the city
That war is over. The destruction of a generation done.

I wonder, what did he do? Did he shout aloud?
He would send the message on to those in charge,
Then maybe he leapt to his feet' cheering with joy,
And the message would spread like flames across oil,
Like the beacons of ancient times. War is over!
Maybe some who had been sent the other news wept
For those who would never come home, sons, lovers,
The husbands who would never father children.
But the Telegrapher; he brought joy inadvertently.
He became a father and a grandfather and on
Roots and branches and leaves of a family tree.
I am quite sure he told the story many times,
Remembered that moment the narrow strip of paper
Unfurled from the reel; the dots and dashes there;
A line drawn visibly under four years of agony,
For his great-great grandson to show in wonder
A full century later to a gathering of friends.

Corfe Castle

She and the dog left the house quietly at sunrise
The air already warm though shadows were long
As they crossed the wide dewy lawn onto The Downs.
Summer heat had made dusty the gorse and heather
Crossed by a web of sandy paths caused by creatures.
Here and there a rabbit-tail hopped out of dog range
And below the roll of heather, the cerulean glass sea.
Larks rose, pouring liquid notes into the cloudless sky,
Until, rounding a sweep of furze, the castle was revealed.
In the hazy air, the battlements appeared intact and ready,
Commanding a dip in the hills and with wide tactical views;
It took nothing to picture the flash of light from helmets;
Snatched echoes of marauding roars and cannon-boom;
To feel the suction of History pulling, pulling, pulling back.

The sounds of the singing ice

It was only when she moved to the lake
Where Winter breathed silver and pearl
Onto the sturdy pines and blades of grass
By the start of November, and the boats
Were beached 'til Spring; where life shrank
Round the fireside, or breath froze on eyelashes;
Only then, as tales and food were shared
Did she hear tell of the sounds sung by the ice.
She checked the science of cracks and laminations.
But then she walked out onto the thickening lake
Lying in fur and mittens, ear pressed through hood
And hat, and Viking hair, hearing the song of the ice.
It could only have been that of water, of Whales,
Of the perfect depth of Winter in the far North
Like the sounds of the Northern Lights in the sky.
Each ancient night she went out on the singing ice
Recording, listening with the bones of her ancestors,
Then making it into her own music; growing old by the lake,
Standing on the shore waiting with joy for the first frost.

For Jonna Jinton

Hunters' Moon

Big wind moon when the surface is cooling
Crops home safely, first frosts' glitter looming;
The month when ancestors brought home meat,
Salted the pork, fired up the smoke-house.
Easy hunting before the savagery of ice and snow
And the axe in the woods led to house repairs,
Stacked and chopped logs and peat by the door.

The days have shrunk and the sunlight thinned,
And the creatures that dive and shriek in the dark
Also prepare. Hedgehogs scuffle and settle in.
This moon is huge, golden through hazed autumnal air.
It reminds our bones of the days of flint and fur
When the Hounds of the Great Hunt bayed and howled
In the October sky, and only the Huntsmen were abroad.

Invalid

If paperwork or laws are termed invalid,
How then does that apply to the warriors
In the hospices, with chemo-blasted immunities
Who smile and fundraise and seize the day?
Or to the Blade Runner and other super humans
Who set records which beat the advantaged ones;
Those who drag out their mask, and glare back
At their demons, every single working day;
To those who walk with their Assistance Dogs
Through crowds more unseeing than they;
Or to genius Hawking with his robot voice,
Unleashed by technology to dazzle the world
And confound the masters of science, rewrite history...
How are these afflicted heroes "invalid" in any way?
Invalids? Rather, they are the champions of the minute,
The hour, the day, where they triumph; and triumph again.

Gone Wild

Unclipped, the verges and wild hedgerows are blooming
Old roses, meadowsweet, hawthorn...billowing scent
Adorned with the Spring natterings of little bird families.
Froths of golden laburnum dangle dancing tails over driveways,
Every shade of lilac and graceful wisteria seduce the senses.
On the edge of the woodland, constellations of wild garlic
Edge the path, and last bluebells still droop in the long grass.
People are absent from this gorgeous unfettered Spring;
The lack of snipping and mowing has encouraged bee
        and butterfly;
The air is filled with birdsong more usually buried by
        roaring traffic.
In city gardens, fox cubs play on the lawns and peep in
        through doors.
Daft goats skip about eating flowers in a deserted Welsh
        seaside town;
Nature is coming out to play, extravagantly dressed
And without supervision.

Billy and the Admiral

Our good friend Billy played the trumpet like a God
It gave him a perfect Cupid's Bow upper lip.
He was a small cheeky bloke who loved the ladies
And twinkled while tooting out effortless soaring jazz.
He liked to reminisce as his age advanced upon him
And had some great tales to tell. He played in the army
And showed me a picture of the boys in uniform
Tooled up with tunes instead of guns, ready to fight
For morale, and keep spirits up. They travelled round,
Charged with this task. But this was not my favourite tale.

Billy worked as a cabinet-maker at the shipbuilders,
Cammell Laird, of Birkenhead. I asked him once
What he had made that he was most proud of;
It was a 12 foot Bird's Eye Maple side board
For the Admiral's Suite, on the immense Ark Royal.
When the Admiral saw it, he asked to meet Billy,
To shake his hand for the beauty of the craftsmanship.
Billy reflected that it sank to the bottom of the sea
When the Ark Royal was torpedoed in 1941.
What a little glimpse of living history! Soon these details
Will no longer be spoken by the cast of the time;
Soon they will be present only on a page, or lost forever.

Second Hand

A perfect book is not pristine, dust cover glossy,
Or the matched noble leather spines in rows
With pages which remain uncut and unread;
A perfect book is one with a further story within
Not merely that of author and publisher,
But those of the reader who left as little
As an exclamation mark that makes you pause
Or as much as detailed annotation, after which
You reread with new eyes, and over again.
It could be a postcard from long ago holidays,
Still sifting sand in the pages creased middles;
A prized post-it note reading "I love you! Xxx"
A stiff congratulatory message or thankyou.
There is the self-evidenced favouritism shown
By a splintered spine repeatedly returned to,
The pages softened by affectionate handling.
Or poems marked by multiple yellow bus tickets
Bought from a Conductor's winding machine
On a bus with an outside spiral staircase and rail.
What price the whisper of another person or time
Tucked up and sleeping until you turn the page?

Grace

Big red-beard man like a Viking, with his Art
For the awkward ones, hands on with all,
Who built his log cabin in the backwoods,
And twinkled at his wife about ugly Death;
But he knew when his time came. Years of meds
Dialysis, increasing struggles, and a choice
Regarding the manner of his own departure.
He knew his own mind, checked with herself,
Was admitted. They made a crazy doorsign
"Enter at your own risk!" and made a wine cart
Which got hidden in the shower from the nurse,
But as he drifted, they came from all around
And kept coming; those she didn't even know he knew;
Colleagues, neighbours, a fellow patient, the lads
Who had smoked and cleared the land with him,
Folks from his Baptist community, all sitting there,
Telling their stories, bringing tokens, playing music.
Registering the Red-sized gap he would leave them.

After two weeks of loving pilgrims, he was gone.
She sat in the Dawn light, then whispered into his ear,
"You lied..." Because friend Death had been so quiet,
Perhaps the gentlest of all. And in her mind, he laughed.

Blue beard

Smiling proprieter of the sunny stubbly fields
And the fairy-lit orchard marquee in the hollow
Where hay bales make siesta space for lanky youngsters
And later serve as benches for crowds of musicians.
You stand on the ridged concrete farmyard
And wave everyone past the pointless gate
With their chairs and coolboxes and blankets
To listen joyously, backlit by stars and the wide sea.
You are the host, with your lively face and blue beard;
Your patchwork waistcoat and smiley eyes miss little.
You seem to measure without judging, to enjoy
What you see with the same humour that made your beard, blue;
That builds this inclusive lively family, built by you.

For Jon Hippy, creator of Folk on the Farm on Ynys Mon

Wildfire

Savage greedy wildfires are gobbling California
Pouncing on trees, roaring in exultant rampages
Crackling through the trees, choking out demon breath
Leaving charred trunks and twigs in its dreadful wake.
Towns like Paradise are reduced to ash and chimneys;
The only heat resistant house parts are the lone survivors.
Along the crumbling highways, fingers of melted engines
Creep from under the bonnets of tyreless blackened cars.
Resistance, or escape, was futile in the face of this furnace.
Eight thousand firefighters battle on, or stand looking down
At what little is left. This is a state sized Crematorium.
How to identify fragments and bones is a colossal conundrum:
Those who were trapped in the safety of their homes, yes.
That is horrific enough. But those who attempted to flee
Will never now leave Paradise. And must somehow be claimed.

Rumplestiltskin

She was one of those women with perfect skin
Pampered by frequent facials and self-indulgence
Yet her heart was gnarled and bitter to the seed.
She would stick out an invisible foot for anyone
In any direction. If they tripped, she smirked.
If they skipped, she could do worse next time.
She was affronted and diminished by others' success
For the expanding of her fellow men made her feel less.

Still there are always those who trip and rise again.
She might put one of those in a windowless barn
With mounds of mouldering straw on every side,
Leave them for weeks on dry bread and stale water
Crushed by the utterly impossible tasks she set.
One of these souls now, they would sit in the dark
And the gilded light of their irrepressibly hopeful heart
Would still turn the blackest of final straws into gold.

The Healing Touch of Music and Water

All of my life, the very heart of me has felt
The healing touch of music and water.
The notes of my throat and of my fingers;
The rich balm of harmony and lovely sounds
That weave like handmade lace, crafted with friends.
Lace and velvet and beautiful beaded silken sounds
Embellishing the feelings of our lives and souls,
Making a moment stretch, and bloom, and pause.

Then there is water; the lakes, the rivers, the sea.
Hushing and swishing along the borders of us,
Shimmering or pounding out powerful drums.
Water has our very nuance and mood.
We are, indeed, made of water as well as dust;
Of salt tears and sweat and liquid blood.
The waves roll and curl, the ripples spread.
Millennia ago, the sea made us. She lays hands
On our tired hearts. And we are stilled.

Upsticks and away

She was ready to leave a full four weeks early
Belongings stripped down, much less savagely
Than the last time, when her treasured hoarded cloth
And instruments of all sorts, and worst of all, her dog,
Had been given away, or long-loaned. That was hard.
She had sold her cabin in the woods, her leafy sanctuary.
That sea was very wide, the life change very great.
Her quarter century of first marriage had been strong
And kind, ended only by death. She had then applied it all
To a man who did not know what love was. She had tried.
But her big heart had learned from grief and adventure;
This was another sea, a different set of losses,
Her life now seemed more like a scattering of boxes
Needing an dusty attic resting place of their very own.

Lime Street

We pull into Lime Street between dripping cliffs of stone
And under the leviathan arch, built by Victorians
Whose vaulting ambitions brought smoke and steam
And post-haste to the farthest corners of Britain.
Travellers no longer dress smartly, or expect staff
To scuttle behind with trunks full of wealth and influence;
There is still pecking order, but now what there is, is business.
Catch the early Pendolino to Euston, and you will see it;
Laptops and cellphones, coffee-fuelled in First Class,
And well into the working day during the journey.
These are the heirs of those who got the railways built
But not of those who built them, nor who dug the canals.

A century and a half later, and this curve of iron and glass
Still shelters and protects. But the building of it did not.
To fling that 200 foot iron span across the hollow air
Meant a fearless crew, who perched on girders with tools
And walked along the rafters like pirates on the plank.
Many will have been Irish, running from the Famine,
Trying to save enough to sail to a classless new start
In America. Far below, the fearsome Gaffer paced,
So the story goes, and when a man slipped high above,
Tumbled yelling to the half-built platform far below
With a sickening thud...this foreman, in his stovepipe hat
And frockcoat, pulled out his pocketwatch, looked,
And said "Clock him off." Done, whether broken or dead.
The heirs of the fallen man sleep on the pavements in the frost
Or work on zero-hours contracts, laid off in a blink;
While gaffers with their cellphones still step over them.

Shiva

White hot and scorching thermo nuclear blast
Vaporising the feelings of anyone in its path
Flattening even the most deeply rooted
Reducing to faint ghostly shadows on walls
Even those who stand further away from it.
Toxic for years, decades; Destroyer of Worlds.
Rage is the careless toy of those who roar in
And out again, leaving behind a wasteland,
Deluded that to explode is a cleansing experience.

Time Out

Somewhere in the limbs that now have knobs,
The papery draped skin that once hugged flesh
There is a long embedded memory of grace.
The movements are hesitant, but gain expression,
As does her face, as she starts to recall dancing.
She surprises herself by being still so supple,
Reaches downwards and curves up and away,
Her head gradually fills with the silken swirl
Of skirt, and dancing backwards in high heels like Ginger,
In strong arms (long gone now) hearts hammering,
Dreaming each others' bright eyes to the music.

But by the time for tea and toast, her creaking joints
Have nudged her back down. She will return again,
Now that she knows where the key to past joys lies.

Jane's Uncle Arthur

Rummaging through a box of white elephant bits,
In among the pottery canapé dishes and moulded glass,
Two tattered black and white photos are stuck together.
And there are two heroic soldiers, World War 2,
In front of a battered canvas tent. Dudes in khaki.
One has military shades, and a tanned lean face,
Sleeves rolled up against the heat, brawny forearms.
Uncle Arthur has a handsome chiselled jaw
Neatly shaved against the Desert sun, eyes shaded
By the peak of his uniform hat. Where are they now,
These heroes of the every-day? Film star looks,
Hearts of lions, given no choice but world travel
To landscapes and battles beyond their wildest dreams.

Old Year/New Year

That time of year when even the lovers
Of beautiful books telling tales of life
And of past lives, flip back to long ago
With all its sad little joys and mighty pangs,
And with trembling fingers turn the tattered leaves
Of memory, weighty and wild and wondrous
With the spicy days of Youth, and old passions
Now congealed like last night's left overs,
Finding fingers sore with sneaky paper cuts
From even a glance at terrible old agonies.

Even these book lovers, with their shredded
Fingers, even they might take a clean blade
And neatly sever and slice out the worst pages;
Maybe put a match to them in the waste-paper bin.
Or maybe they might love the books too much
And leave all of it there, for some-one else to read.

Holocaust Day

It struck her like the grip of ice round her heart
That had the roulette wheel of time and history
Dropped her in 1939, rather than the safer 2019,
There was no way that she could have escaped.
Her tribe; the artists, the free thinkers who question,
Those who challenge the rules and do not follow
The beckoning finger of others who wield power;
Who value kindness over wealth. And not just that.
The condition of her health would have listed her
As incurable, progressively sick, a burden on the state.

They would have collected her. It was she in the train
Blasted by cold through the slats intended for cows.
And when she arrived, no point in making her work.
Herded across mud by men with the hearts of machines
To where the looming chimney smoked night and day
With black ash and fear and countless souls. It was us all.

Oxford Librarian

He is dapper and bearded and spectacled
Just as one might hope, with autumn hair
Tied back, a venerable leather briefcase.
His equally long-haired and fabulous ginger cat
Travels on his shoulder each day on the bus.

In the elegant columnular peace of his domain
The cat pads round with a gorgeous plume of tail
Permitting tucked-away students to pay court
Until, finally, coiling on his favourite shelf
Where his liquid amber eyes slowly drift closed.
No-one doubts to whom the College library belongs.
Least of all the students, the staff or the librarian.

Primavera

Heal my heart with the touch of your warm fingers
Reaching to where I sleep in my warm blanket of soil.
Tickle the tangled roots and bulbs 'til they wake
And shake out their green bonnets for the parade.
Where you walk, first snowdrops unfurl fragile petals;
Early tiny blossoms make Oriental elegance of bare boughs;
Sassy dandelions cackle in the lawn, ready to feed the bees.
Everyone is drawn out. They chat, they stroll, they mow.
Hawthorn leaves erupt in lively twittering hedgerows.
There are smiles. There is colour. We are all reborn.

A Bit of Hush

All night we watched the bloke by the door
Get up and down, up and down, up and down,
With every coming and going of ladies to the loo
And beer carrying musicians into the parlour,
Where hard benches lined the uneven walls
And the ships' plank floors of the room above
Were so low you could reach them. Each person
Arrived or left; the old door swung open; up he got
To stuff a folded beermat in to keep the bar chat out.
His patience was amazing and pointless and kind
To the quieter singers in the room. He only gave up
When the music became stronger than the jollity...
Ceased his little comedy with a self-deprecating shrug
Leaving a pile of folded beermats on each side of the door.

Wedding Dress

The day they got the telegram he had survived
Having bailed from his burning Spitfire over fields
Was beyond reality. She sat in the garden weeping
With joy, in her ugly utilitarian clothes, home-made
From scrimped clothing coupons, and made wishes
For a fine frock to hurl herself into his returning arms in.

On the day, the smell of each others' skin mattered more
Than fine feathers. Kisses on kisses, tears, greedy eyes,
Then they sat while he told his incredible tale. By his feet
In his battered kit bag, he revealed the ruched treasure
Of the precious parachute that had floated him home.
She lifted it out, yards upon yards of petal-soft silk,
That had saved his life, and now meant her moment
Of beauty. She left the underpinnings of the billows
And straps, and made a crinoline, like Scarlett O'Hara,
And stood at the head of the aisle with brimming eyes
In her perfect dress made of life saved, and life to come.

The wedding dress is in the Museum of Toronto

Botanical

Two elderly sisters had lived quietly together
In their tall echoing house on the road to the shore.
Inside, the chairs stood about in corners unsat on;
A drift of dust settled on a number of unused beds.
There were hats on the hall stand for heads long gone
And bell pushes for servants who would never answer.

But outside; now, that was a different tale of wonder!
The huge back garden showed the flourish of their art;
In the greenhouse, one Miss Myers fed her precious babies,
Talked quietly to them as she pottered in their company.
Every corner brimmed with colour. There were maples
By a Chinese bridge like the ones on the plates, flame leafed.
A tiny waterfall and a lily pond, and borders of shapely things.
In the kitchen garden there were apple trees like ladders,
And furthermost was a meadow of swishy blonde grass
And wild poppies. The ladies loved their plants with a passion
But most of all they loved it when the children knocked,
And came through to patter along the gravel paths exclaiming
In joy and wonder at the beauty of their masterpiece.

Little Visitors

Through the glass doors there are warm wards.
Beeping machines keep watch in quiet rooms,
Staff walk on soft shoes with kind steady steps.
They all know, yet do not say, there is a dim-lit hall
Where flutters of gossamer butterflies flit and play;
Flickering wings just out of sight, half-heard voices,
Of little ones who hover at the last point of contact,
Fading with time yet flocking, keeping company.
Sometimes, feet will patter, a wisp of song or laughter,
Heard by all the staff, more so when the moon is full,
But mostly not discussed, or feared, just absorbed
With the agony of the parents who are left behind.

Bidston

Up a crumbling road called Wilding Way
The smoke-blackened monument stands proud.
The Lighthouse is next door, the light of which
Aligned with Leasowe Light to guide ships in.
All these are now their own Epitaph; and their own tales.

The Observatory is astonishing. The two white domes
Command Wirral from the ridge, and even yet inside them
The cogs and handles can still turn the whole dome
And open a broad slot, like a slice of stars from edge to edge.
The experts who worked here had knowledge of Time and Tide
And did the calculations to plan the D-Day Landings.
And deep into the solid rock below the weight of this
Lies a strange abandoned cellar where overturned chairs
And desks are all that remain of a Zero Gravity Laboratory
Where mysterious data was created and gathered
For use in space. How is this marvellous relic not revered?
It should be open as a museum, full of school children
Doing guided Tours and feeling the breath of History
In their ear, who would leave with an altered perspective
About their local landscape. Instead, it is a grotty hostel
For experts from across the world, come to work data,
And around them this wonderful building slowly falls apart.

The Observatory has since been bought and is in use for Arts courses

Oysters

Flapping around on the floor of the ocean
Is a gritty affair. The outer shell gets gnarled,
Turns to clamped armour sadly inefficient
Against wealthy aphrodisiac seekers' greed
Who fling your live lemon-drenched flesh
Down their open throats. Fresh, they say.
Should you escape that, there is grit.
Then, there are those who coat their grit
Layer upon tenacious layer, for year on year,
And make radiant pearls out of their pain.

Sea Salt

Childhood holidays were on Ynys Mon, or Anglesey,
Where they played on wide open white beaches
Among plentiful shells, and splashed in shallows
Where the sunlight flickered across tiny tickly fish
And translucent scuttly crabs. Picnics were gritty,
And ice cream came from a tin shack. Sun shone.

But one storm-wracked day before Health and Safety
Shrivelled the possibilities for awfully big adventures,
Her and her brothers were entrusted to an old Sea Salt
To search for seals in his robust rowing boat, over waves
Like walls of water. They clung in a clump in the stern,
Staring up the tilted length of the boat at his brawny arms
And tanned sturdy hands on the worn wooden oars.
He knew his waters and their wild winds: they did see seals
And came back safely with wild hair and wild eyes into harbour.

Forty years later, she passed by Moelfre Lifeboat Station
And saw their Captain in Life sized statue form, still salty
And windswept, memorialised for 50 years preserving lives.
They had been safe in the brave hands of Richard Evans;
They had searched for seals in a storm with a legend.

Food Banks and Ferraris

The shop doorways are not the same,
Not in any way, in a first-world country,
Where tattered ex-servicemen are lost,
Diverted from main stream life by horrors
They absorbed in the line of duty, and now
Sleep in the frost of any unshuttered doorway.
The streets are not the same. Even the towns.
Or where a couple with three jobs take kids
To queue at the food bank, and dress in cast-offs.
A few miles away, there is an obscene gold Ferrari
Plonked arrogantly on the double yellows at will,
Displaying the benefit of Tax-Haven banking
With peacock conspicuousness. Look at me,
It says; look at me. Hard work does deserve reward,
But it seems that dignity and taste are no longer in fashion,
Perhaps along with team-work and honesty and kindness.

Make-up drawer

Mother's dressing table was classic Art Deco
With a huge mirror, two side columns of drawers
And a wide central drawer of perfumed treasures.
Open it, and scent of glamour pouffed into the air;
Face powder in a flat compact, Tweed and Blue Grass,
Lippy and diamante bits and bobs. The scent bottle
With a silky pink bubble to squeeze, a cigarette case,
Gloves, long pearl beads, big clip-on earrings.

And in the fat wardrobe, where the door squeaked,
There were padded hangers with little lavender bags,
And more treasures; wide collars, swishy fifties skirts.
A few years later there would be crushed velvet Kaftans,
And a purple velvet evening gown with a gold bodice.
And always there, underlying, the scent of Mother.

Cathedral

Look upwards past the soaring pillars
Be they of carved stone or breathing wood;
Be the perfect vault made of man's ingenuity
Or of tender leaves leading to cerulean blue;
Each will have lasted years upon years.

Generations have bloomed and faded
While Notre Dame towered over the Seine
Perched on 800 year old fantasy buttresses
Like dragon's legs. Yet when her roof burned
Few oak trees remained which were old enough
To put back her rafters. Old Oak is as hard as stone
And yet, it burned. It is lopped to make bypasses
And Business parks, and the beautiful lungs
Of the Earth are vanishing. But find you a green wood
Where the bird choirs echo in the clear air, gaze upwards
To the sky, and go homewards having glimpsed Heaven.

Tower of Strength

After the work load he had thought never to clear
Had been swirled out of the fractured windows,
He watched while panic enveloped his colleagues.
The screens on every desk and wall were blank and dark.
Sparks hissed from wiring and water from sprinklers.
Still he sat at his desk while time echoed and stilled.
Once in a while, a person fell past outside from above
And vanished into the smoke and ash billowing up.
There was no one for him to call. No wife or children.

The girders of the glittering tower creaked around him.
Somehow, in the end, he got up and opened the door
Into the deserted hallway. The weight of the fire door
To the stairs seemed impossible. Shrieks and smoke
Echoed up the hollow space. He started downwards.
After a few floors, a girl in bare feet and a sharp suit
Sobbed into her mobile and refused to come with him.
After a few more, with crashing above him and below,
He also sat down and leaned against the tipping wall.
He could make no sense of events or of his choices.
The Smoke was in his head now, and in his closing chest.

And then there was a cough, not human, and a big dog
Was somehow licking his face. Nudging him, pulling;
Tumbling down the collapsing stairwell through dust
And staggering finally across the road, as behind them
The Towers roared and bellowed into oblivion.

For Daisy, Assistance Dog to James Crane, who worked on floor
112 of the World Trade Centre, and voluntarily returned 3 times,
saving 967 people in total. She was given the Medal of Honor of
New York City, and survived, being carried out by firefighters with
burns and multiple injuries.

Invisible Witness

Twenty years of ladders and buckets,
Announcing his arrival with a dull thud
Of ladder on wall, he knows them all.
His warm heart has fetched bread and milk,
Searched for lost cats, cleared the fog,
But the window cleaner knows more;
He sees the anger and the grief and the loneliness;
The old ones who stare silently into space,
The crash and burn of broken marriages,
The teenager alone in front of a vast TV.
He sees affection and chuckles and family life,
Home improvements and disintegration.
On the other side of the glass he is cloaked
In the invisibility of accustomed familiarity;
Apart, yet also a part of the daily life of them all.

Scape Goat

How heavy and breathless the cut of the wire
Of the thunderous weight, giant stone blocks dragging,
Pulling through muscle and organ. All the agonies
Of the World, shouldered by those who cannot help
Or avoid that privilege, that dreaded leaden weight
Of lost children, lost love, pain, illness, disillusions...
Outcast on the sun-blasted desert sands, lugging
A pyramid of escalating sins and anguishes, beyond
Impossible blocks of others' pain; so much worse
Than ever could be one's own. Beyond worse.

Made new

His first dim awareness was of the strong perfume
Of heavy spices, and cloth, and dank stone and sand.
His eyes showed blind darkness. His chin was bound.
Even so, his limbs were warm and supple. He reached
To unbind, to untangle, to sort out his loose clothing,
Swung his legs round from the rough sleeping platform
And got the first flashback of agony and hostile shouts;
Of stumbling with ragged feet across hot stone; of weight
Across the raw flesh of his shoulders. He drew in a breath
And there was now no pain. Fingers flexed, shoulders back,
Feet down onto the sandy floor. He followed the rough wall
With his hands. There was a clear doorway, low, blocked,
Yet when he pushed, the first roseate light of Dawn peeped.
A bloom of joy flushed in his heart. He pushed again, harder.
Light flooded the chamber; it was as if he was helped
By bright unseen hands, that cupped his elbows, led him.
There was some early mist among the ancient Olive trees,
Where goat bells clanked. He sat on a rock with new limbs;
Touched the skin of his face and marvelled. And waited
With a calm elated heart for those who would soon come.

Choices

They had set about their sea change with typical care
But that meant being parted by work and wide miles
And in that year, they both worried about their choice.
There was also the problem of gilded French Furniture
And many fine paintings, and a whole library of books
To squish into a Welsh cottage. And funding concerns.
But then, their measured steps led them both to home.

Gone was the autocracy of work, the misery of separation;
Instead, the shifting sea for the full width of the horizon,
Washing snapping and dancing on the line, time to read,
Discovering peeping snowdrops under the twirly ivy.
She sat back on her heels in the garden one clear day
And watched him bringing tea towards her, eyes crinkly
With the smile that never now was missing; and was content.

Tribal

Open the door and walk down a bland hallway
Then into a world of quiffs and coloured lights
Wide swishy skirts and waists and perky busts;
Leopard prints, romantic roses and polka dots,
Where the modern take on fifties womankind
Includes tattoos and foxy shoes and scarlet lips.
The men are peacocks in spats and Bowling shirts
Playfully swaggering for frequent smoking breaks
While the DJ spins Vintage Vinyl with its warmer tone
Before the bands step up. No backing tracks here;
A veteran Country band bangs out Johnny Cash
Before the Headliners, proudly launching their album,
With a babyfaced Slap Bass player dude in Creepers
Drummer laying down a runaway Rockabilly groove;
Master-craftsman guitarist, smiley pretty singeress.
Not just the playing, but the good nature is a time slip;
A form of hip tribalism packed with fun and nostalgia.

Dusk

Earlier in the day he had queued for soup and a coat
Handed out by volunteers, who took the time to connect,
Smiling kindly. The extra layer of padding was good
Holding the warmth of the food and covering his craggy bones.
A lucky snag of some boxes kept him off the cobbles, knees up,
Staring at busy legs and feet as streams of people rushed past him
Laden with bags. Somewhere not too far away a brass band played
Solid traditional horns and a harmony choir doing Christmas songs.

Once in a while, a hand would come down with a hot cup of coffee
And once some youngsters brought him a paper bag of chips and burger.
He continued to exist. The lively crowds thinned out, shops shut.
The day was dimming now, and the cold starting to bite.
He curled up in his chosen doorway. Darkness and quiet
Swept down the deserted street, past the stacked bin bags
Waiting for morning collection, swirled in the skeletal trees.
Dusk finally reduced his fragile abandoned frame to refuse
When the pity-filled faces of the bin men found him at first light.

The Furthest Summit

Green fields are lovely in a juicy, safe way,
And the dappled shade of the woodland
With the glorious scent of Bluebells
Rising through the senses like a wave;
The pebbled shore, wave-ridged ripples,
Sand-swirls hazing the dropping sun.
Life's landscapes have all these lovely things.

But it is conquering our looming mountains
Which marks us most painful and marvellous,
Which makes us heroes to ourselves.
Cliffs and sliding scree, finger holds, overhangs,
Breath burning the lungs, muscles grunting,
Topping the rise to see in the distance yet another.
Draw breath, pull up from the ribs, plod on
Under wide skies full of pink mackerel clouds,
Along a knife-edge ridge, flanked by the Abyss,
To stand breathless at the cairn, to place your rock
On a pile with others' achievements, and look out;
To know, at last, that you stand undefeated,
And to say aloud, "I can, and I did."

Old Peculiar

The tall stools stand empty along the mahogany bar;
Low brass lights make little vertical pools of gold;
The copper drip trays and ceramic pump handles
Go back to a century when this was the tap room
Or a coaching inn on a muddy lane into the Dale.
There is a stillness in time here which has outlasted
Two World Wars and seismic social upheavals.
In the Ladies' Lounge, respectfully extended,
Congenial groups have gathered to eat and chat.
Each heavy table sits on its own oriental rug
And the old parquet floor is gleaming.

In the Tap Room, a solitary large man perches,
Overflowing the stool seat. His shoulders hunch.
Whatever home he has slipped out of for a quick pint
Visibly fails to draw him. Wealth weighs him down;
He is isolated among the jokes and anecdotes of others
Staring into the murky depths of his Old Peculiar.

Drag Diva

Your lost sad eyes half covered by the wide brim of your hat
And long gloves concealed possible tattoos on your arms.
Your frock was understated and flattering to your frame
Your stance was poised, and only your height hinted
At another story. You were alone in your fashion parade;
A catwalk of elegance that passed us by throughout the day.
Your only purpose seemed to sampling differing versions
Of alternative identities. As the dusk settled and softened
The tatty hotels and bars, I watched you lug your cases
Out to your car, dressed once more in faceless Denim.
Bags were not the true sad weight which dragged you down
As you packed yourself away and wearily headed off
Without your Race Day glamour, back to faded Denim days.

Waiting

Perfect foxgloves leaned on the warm ancient stone
Of the Cathedral walls. The uneven flagstoned paths
Had settled with gentle undulations over the tree roots,
And in the Nave, sunlit moments peered through glass
Making blurred patterns on vault and arch and banner.
The rows of seats filled up. The organist flexed the pipes.
Out of sight, the Ordinands reflected on discarded lives
Weighed their choices, felt humbled by the support.
Her excitement fluttered and bubbled inside her,
And when she went forth to the fanfare of the choir
And felt the blessings of them all, that smile burst out
Dazzling everyone in sight, showering joy onto them all.

For Rev Ailsa Whorton 15/06/20

Remember

There are no winners in wars, however just
Or justified, by those who loom over maps
At a safe distance. Propaganda blares out
For all the gladiators, bullying, directing fear,
Making the other lads demons, dead even so;
Just bloodied heaps of frightened boys and men
Down the long and shameful history of humans,
Leaving widows, and orphans, and spinsters. And Pride.

War's savage wastelands are made out of honour;
Determination to defend and protect. Hardest of all,
Going over the top into the gunfire, fighting comrades
Who yesterday sung carols and kicked a football about
In the grisly blast holes and barbed wire of No Man's Land.

Wilderness

I take my tattered heart through the cool woods
Where the shade-freckled ivy drapes, and moths dance
In bars of fading light finding their exact way downwards.
While the sun blasts the heath and the dried-out fields,
Each little clearing offers more gentle seasonal glimpses;
Fat brambles, apricot confectioner-curls of Honeysuckle,
My kind friend the old Oak flutters a leaf onto my hand,
And further along the narrow path through wild raspberries,
Where the memory of the perfumed Bluebells of Spring
Whispers hope into my ear, an angel feather flutters down
Seemingly from nowhere, turning and floating on the quiet air;
Unconditional absolution, acceptance, a measure of peace.

East o' Hills

Leaving their explosive neighbours behind
With their invasive anger and their fisticuffs,
They moved themselves to God's Little Acre
To sit in the monastic peace of the green garden
Next to a singing bamboo and a crimson Acer.
What joy for their hearts to feel so safe and calm
Where once a Holy Man had tilled the good earth
And his chickens had gossiped and pecked
Along the rows of vegetables. Kindness stayed.

Centuries later, when the acre of land was sold
And a neat close of town houses in light brick
Tucked behind the ancient sandstone cottage,
Many of those who were drawn in felt that kindness.
It settled them into their homes and with their neighbours.
And the birdsong in the quiet dusk might have been
From centuries before, heard as he leaned on his hoe.

The Art of Precious Scars

The bowl he had dropped a week ago
Lay stacked, shard upon shard, on his bench.
There was little remarkable about it, even whole,
Save that it had shared his journey and that of his parents.
Now he had time. First was the pre-op inspection;
Then the plan, forensic in detail, examining each
And every irregular piece, laying them out flat,
Preparing the reconstruction. Then, at last,
The process itself. The shape slowly re-emerged
Like an old friend, reborn in his dusty craftsman's hands.

Next morning at first light, he looked at the puckered scar
On his strong survivor of a wife, where her dear flesh
Had been through a similar destructive process.
He left her Sleeping peacefully, and when he gilded the cracks
On the salvaged dish, wished he could do the same for her.

Kintsugi is the Japanese art of repairing pottery with gold,
sometimes referred to as "The Art of Precious Scars"

Island

When I go, let it be on my precious island
In a great wooden ship like my ancestors
With a white-hot heart to the greedy fire
And savage roaring wind-whipped flames
Streaming bright veils of glowing sparks
Upwards into the velvet midnight sky.
Let there be tales and songs, spoken and sung,
By any there who still remain to love me,
While the curlews whistle on the sandbanks
And sleepy seals call their siren songs.

Stay out there in the starlight, my friends.
Wake with the sun, be glad of waking,
And walk back as the tide permits you
Away from the charred boat, with quiet hearts
Over the ridged sand, over the coarse grass,
Back to your lives, with hearts still spark-touched.